Alfred's Instrumental CD+ Play-Along

Alto Saxophone   **Level 1**

Easy Instrumental Solos for Special Occasions & Celebrations

MW00581176

Contents

MP3 CD Track

Arranged by Bill Galliford, Ethan Neuburg, and David Pugh.
Recordings produced by Dan Warner, Doug Emery, Lee Levin, Bill Galliford, and Ethan Neuburg.

Alfred Music
P.O. Box 10003
Van Nuys, CA 91410-0003
alfred.com

ISBN-10: 1-4706-1920-2
ISBN-13: 978-1-4706-1920-6

Track 2: Demo
Track 3: Play-Along

AULD LANG SYNE

Words by
ROBERT BURNS

Traditional Carol

WE SHALL OVERCOME

Track 4: Demo
Track 5: Play-Along

Adaptation by
GUY CARAWAN, FRANK HAMILTON,
ZILPHIA HORTON and PETE SEEGER

SHE LOVES YOU

Track 6: Demo
Track 7: Play-Along

Words and Music by
JOHN LENNON and PAUL McCARTNEY

Bright rock (♩ = 152)

DANNY BOY (LONDONDERRY AIR)

Words by
FREDERIC WEATHERLY

Traditional Irish Aire

Slowly (♩ = 72)

THE IRISH WASHERWOMAN

Traditional Irish Folk Song

Track 10: Demo
Track 11: Play-Along

I'D LIKE TO TEACH THE WORLD TO SING

Words and Music by
BILL BACKER, ROQUEL DAVIS,
ROGER COOK and ROGER GREENAWAY

Track 12: Demo
Track 13: Play-Along

BECAUSE HE LIVES

Words by
WILLIAM J. and GLORIA GAITHER

Music by
WILLIAM J. GAITHER

*E♯ = F♮

PETER COTTONTAIL

Track 16: Demo
Track 17: Play-Along

Words and Music by
JACK ROLLINS and STEVE NELSON

CIELITO LINDO

Track 18: Demo
Track 19: Play-Along

Traditional Mexican Song

Cielito Lindo - 2 - 1

A MOTHER'S PRAYER

Track 20: Demo
Track 21: Play-Along

Words and Music by
DAVID FOSTER and CAROLE BAYER SAGER

Slowly and gently (♩ = 74)

YOU RAISE ME UP

Track 22: Demo
Track 23: Play-Along

Words and Music by
ROLF LOVLAND and BRENDAN GRAHAM

TRUMPET TUNE

Track 24: Demo
Track 25: Play-Along

Composed by
HENRY PURCELL

rit.

POMP AND CIRCUMSTANCE

Track 26: Demo
Track 27: Play-Along

Composed by
SIR EDWARD ELGAR

AMERICA THE BEAUTIFUL

Track 28: Demo
Track 29: Play-Along

Words and Music by
SAMUEL WARD

Moderately slow (♩ = 88)

31

SUMMERTIME
(from *Porgy and Bess*)

Music and Lyrics by
GEORGE GERSHWIN,
DuBOSE and DOROTHY HEYWARD
and IRA GERSHWIN

Track 30: Demo
Track 31: Play-Along

THIS LAND IS YOUR LAND

Words and Music by
WOODY GUTHRIE

THE CHICKEN DANCE
(DANCE LITTLE BIRD)

Track 34: Demo
Track 35: Play-Along

Music by
TERRY RENDALL and
WERNER THOMAS

Moderately bright (♩ = 168)

FUNERAL MARCH OF A MARIONETTE

Composed by
CHARLES GOUNOD

Track 36: Demo
Track 37: Play-Along

Moderately (♩. = 92)

*A♯ = B♭

COME, YE THANKFUL PEOPLE, COME

Words by
HENRY ALFORD

Music by
GEORGE J. ELVEY

rit.

AWAY IN A MANGER (MEDLEY)

Track 40: Demo
Track 41: Play-Along

Music by
JAMES R. MURRAY (1887) and
WILLIAM J. KIRKPATRICK

Away in a Manger (Medley) - 2 - 1

Away in a Manger (Medley) - 2 - 2

JINGLE BELLS

Track 42: Demo
Track 43: Play-Along

Words and Music by
JAMES PIERPONT

Moderately fast (♩ = 144)

(♩ = 72 This represents the song pulse feel counted in two.)

YOU'RE A MEAN ONE, MR. GRINCH

(from *How the Grinch Stole Christmas*)

Track 44: Demo
Track 45: Play-Along

Lyrics by
DR. SEUSS

Music by
ALBERT HAGUE

I HAVE A LITTLE DREIDEL

Track 46: Demo
Track 47: Play-Along

Traditional Hanukkah

Moderately bright (♩ = 144)

HAPPY BIRTHDAY TO YOU

Track 48: Demo
Track 49: Play-Along

Words and Music by
MILDRED J. HILL and PATTY S. HILL

PARTS OF AN ALTO SAXOPHONE AND FINGERING CHART

• When there are two fingerings given for a note, use the first one unless the alternate fingering is suggested.

• When two enharmonic notes are given together (F♯ and B♭ for example,) they sound the same pitch and are played the same way.

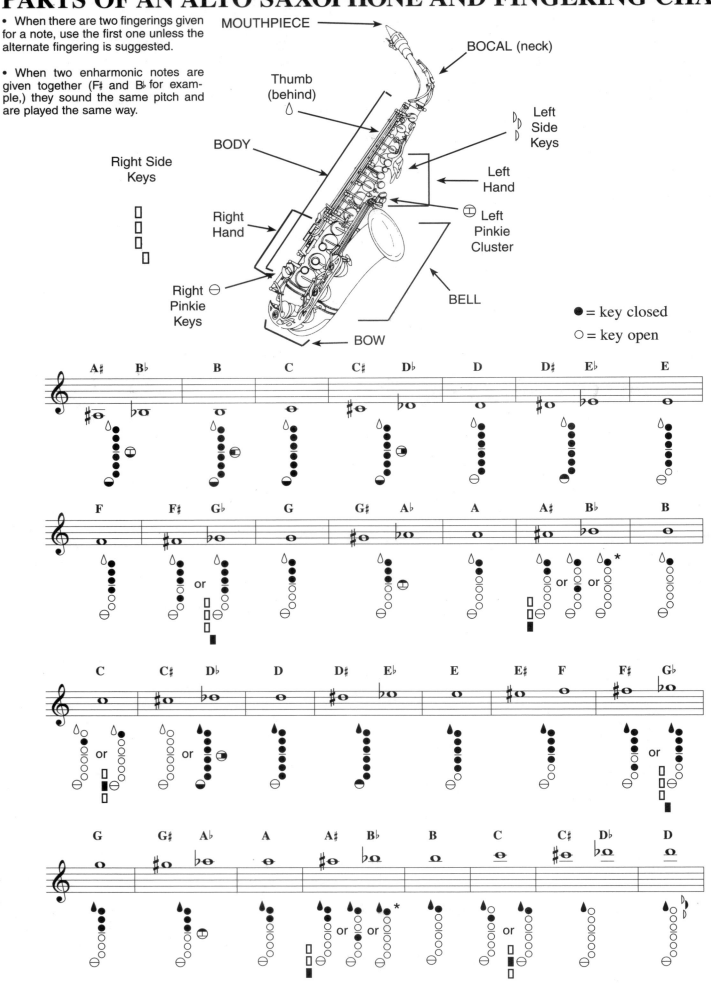

* Both pearl keys are pressed with the Left Hand 1st finger.